AF867537

Autism Self-Discovery Companion

Unmask. Explore. Create.

LiL Penguin Studios

Title: Autism Self-Discovery Companion
Copyright © 2026 by Vadas Réka
LiL Penguin Studios
All rights reserved.
Published by LiL Penguin Studios
Written and illustrated by Réka Vadas, creator of LiL Penguin Studios

No part of this publication may be reproduced, stored in a retrieval system, transmitted, distributed, or shared in any form or by any means-electronic, mechanical, photocopying, recording, scanning, or otherwise-without prior written permission from the copyright holder, except for brief quotations used in reviews or where permitted by copyright law.
The text, illustrations, characters, designs, layouts, and other original content in this book are protected by copyright.
This publication may not be copied, scanned, uploaded, redistributed, or used to train, develop, fine-tune, or improve artificial intelligence (AI), machine learning models, datasets, or other generative AI technologies without the express written permission of the copyright holder.

ISBN 978-615-02-7514-7
First paperback edition 2026

Disclaimer

The author is not a healthcare professional. This book is based on lived autistic experience and is intended for educational, creative, and self-reflection purposes only. It is not a substitute for professional medical, psychological, therapeutic, or legal advice, diagnosis, or treatment.
Autism is a diverse spectrum, and every autistic person experiences it differently. The examples, illustrations, prompts, and activities in this book are intended to encourage exploration and reflection, not to define what autism should look like. If you have questions about your health or well-being, please seek guidance from an appropriately qualified professional.

Some material in this book has been adapted from content originally published at the author's website: lilpenguinstudios.com.

Hi!

Hello!

Hello!

Hi!

Hi!

Hello!

Hello!

Hi!

Hi!

Hello!

This Book Is Yours!

Keep every page private,
share one page, or share a few.
It is completely up to you.

If you'd like to share your pages, artwork, or favorite creations—or simply see what others have made, use the hashtag:

#LiLPenguinCompanions

or

Explore LiL Penguin's World at:

lilpenguinstudios.com

This book belongs to...

☆ Name:

☆ Favorite color:

☆ Favorite animal:

☆ Current special interest:

☆ Favorite comfort item:

☆ Favorite stim:

☆ Favorite snack:

Before You Begin

Use your favorite art supplies, pencils, pens, washi tapes, stickers, and more!

Just give them a quick test on the next page first.

Different supplies behave differently on different papers, and wetter materials may wrinkle the pages or show through.

Test & Swatch

Contents

What kind of book is this?

Honestly?
A little bit of everything.
A visual guide.
A journal.
A scrapbook.
A creative space.
A collection of experiences.
A place to learn, reflect, create, and explore.

This isn't a book that tells you what autism is.
It's a place to discover what autism looks like for you.

Some pages explain.
Some pages ask questions.
Some pages give you space to draw, write, doodle, decorate, and tell your story.
Some pages might make you think:
'Wait... that's so me.'
Others might make you think:
'Actually... not me.'
And that's the point. There is no single autistic experience.
You're not more or less autistic because of it.

Use it your way.
Fill every page. Skip pages.
Come back later.
Cover it in stickers, notes, sketches, and random thoughts.
Make it neat.
Make it chaotic.
Make it completely yours.

Because when you're done, this won't just be a book about autism. It will be a snapshot of you.
Your experiences.
Your strengths.
Your challenges.
Your needs.
Your joys.
Your interests.
Your comfort items.
Your communication style.
Your way of moving through the world.

No two copies should look the same.
Because no two autistic people are the same.

This is your space.
Your story.
Your autistic self.
And that's where everything starts.

Gentle Reminder

Some examples fit.
Others don't.

Both can help you find the words
for your own experience.

The goal isn't to fit the book.

The goal is for the book to fit you.

Let's Start!

Autism is a spectrum
NOT like this
very autistic? No!
a little bit autistic? No!
But like this
We're both autistic...
...but we have different strengths and difficulties
social skills
communication
repetitions
executive function
interests
perception
sensitivities
other
LiL Penguin Studios

Your spectrum

Color and label areas where you need more or less support.

Easily Overlooked Autistic Traits

Easily Overlooked Autistic Traits

Sensory issues

Often overlooked as

-just overreacting

Reality

-your needs matter

-it's important to use accommodations to prevent overstimulation if possible

How to help

-be patient, provide a sensory friendly environment

-in case of overstimulation, help to find a way out of the situation/place

What are your biggest sensory 'yeses' and 'nos'?
Write, doodle, add stickers, or make a collage.

Easily Overlooked Autistic Traits

Executive function problems

Often overlooked as

-just being lazy

Reality

-it's hard, you wanna do it but have no idea how to start, what steps to take

-there are so many ways that simple tasks can be overwhelming

How to help

-give clear instructions

-use visual tools

-help to organize & identify the required steps

What little victories are you proud of?
Write, doodle, add stickers, or make a collage.

Easily Overlooked Autistic Traits

Missing social cues

Often overlooked as

-just being rude

Reality

-you're trying your best, you mean well, and that's what really matters.
-being rude is not an autistic trait.
-autistic people as any other people can be rude but that has nothing to do with autism

How to help

-be straightforward
-do not give hints

Make a list of things you wish came with instructions.
(situations, conversations, daily life... anything!)

Easily Overlooked Autistic Traits

Comfort items

Often overlooked as

-just being childish

Reality

-they're amazing
-autistic people can be attached to objects much more easily
-they can help in overwhelming situations & make you feel safe

How to help

- accept it
-normalize it

Draw, collage, or list your comfort item(s). Then surround them with words they bring to mind.

Easily Overlooked Autistic Traits

Special interests

Often overlooked as

-just being obsessed
-just being a geek

Reality

they are vital for autistic people
-provide a safe space
-help in self-regulation

How to help

- know that special interest info dump is an autistic love language
-never make fun of them

Special Interest Overload

Cover this page with anything and everything about your special interest.

Easily Overlooked Autistic Traits

Going nonspeaking in certain situations

Often overlooked as

just being shy

Reality

not being able to talk in certain situations

How to help

- do not pressure
- accept nonverbal forms of communication

It would help...

Write small things that would be an ease
when it's hard to talk: a person, a fictional character,
a place, words, comfort items, a song, anything.

Autism & Fluctuating Support Needs

Autism & Fluctuating Support Needs

Autistic support needs fluctuate during a person's life, from year to year, week to week, day to day. It doesn't mean that you are more or less autistic on one day or the other.

Fluctuating support needs are part of being autistic.

Autistic masking, autistic burnout, environmental changes, daily challenges, personal experiences and many other things can affect it heavily.

It's important to be patient with yourself or your autistic loved ones and always ask for professional help if you need it.

Some days need more support. Some days need less. Both are okay.

Autism & Fluctuating Communication

you might be able to talk about your special interest for hours

but go nonspeaking when overwhelmed

When words just flow...

When words hide...

Collect words,
emojis, stickers, or doodles that match each side.

Autism & Fluctuating Sensitivities

you might be able to handle hearing an irritating sound in the afternoon

but you might have a meltdown when hearing the same sound early in the morning

Sensory Treasure Hunt

Collect your sensory treasures.
Things that help when everything
feels too loud, too bright, or too much.

Autism & Fluctuating Energy Levels

you might be able to socialize and work a lot on one day

but you might be barely able to get out of bed on the next day

Things I can do on high-energy days...

Things I can still do on low-energy days...

Autism & Fluctuating Interoception

you might be able to tell
that it's hot one day

but have no idea what's wrong
when you're boiling in your
wool sweater the next day

I wish I came with notifications...

What would yours say? Maybe 'You're thirsty!', 'Take a break!', 'You're getting cold!', or something different.
Fill this page with your own notifications.

Autism & Fluctuating Special Interests

Having a special interest feels like...

Autism & Fluctuating Executive Functioning

you might be able to go shopping on one day

but don't know how to get dressed or put a meal on a plate on the other

Doing my best looks different every day

Fill this page with your small wins.

Maybe getting dressed, brushing your teeth, taking a break, making food, drinking water or something completely different.

Autistic Masking

Autistic Masking

Forcing eye contact

Autistic Masking

Coordinating body language and facial expressions even though it's incredibly exhausting

to make up for missing social cues and somehow lessen further misunderstandings.

I can be completely myself...

I mask a little...

I fully mask...

Fill each section with people, places, little things you do, words, doodles, or collages.

Autistic Masking

because you learned that 'it's not that bad/loud/bright', etc.

Let's do it!

Things I want to say when I need to....

Autistic Masking

•The Ultimate Brain Dump•

Autistic Masking

Rehearsing conversations and scripting in advance

in order to be able
to speak and
have that conversation at all.

Script Twist

Fill this page with **quotes from your favorite character** in your comfort movie, TV show, or book.

Autistic Unmasking

They might look like simple objects...

But they might be the only thing that can help.

This or That?

Chewing gum — Chewelry
Sunglasses — Cap
Earplugs — Headphones
Fidget toy — Soft fabric
Bare feet — Socks
Plushie — Weighted blanket
Tight clothes — Loose clothes
Sunshine — Rain
Summer — Winter
Chair — Floor seat
Nature trip — City walk
Morning — Night

Autistic Unmasking

Giving yourself time to...

recharge after overwhelming situations

stim & enjoy sensory play

your special interests

recover after shutdowns/meltdowns

take a break after a hyperfocus loop

adjust to any change

rest on low energy days

take it slow during an autistic burnout

and not measuring yourself to neurotypical standards

Permissions I'd like to give myself...

Types of Stimming

Lil Penguin Studios

Spot Your Stims

Tactile

soft plushies

fidget toys

petting an animal

walking on grass

hair twirling

playing in water

feeling the wind

bean bags

Visual

lining up objects

glitter & sparkles

candle light

cloud gazing

kaleidoscopes

hourglasses

snow globes

observing shadows

switching lights on & off

Vestibular & Proprioceptive

slides

bouncing

hand flapping

swings

rocking

hanging upside down

trampolines

spinning

pacing

twirling

Auditory

- wave sounds
- making tapping sounds
- listening to the same song
- clicking pens
- snapping fingers
- rain sounds
- fireplace sounds
- fans

Taste & Smell

- sniffing books
- scented candles
- crunchy foods
- chewing gum
- smelling objects

Vocal

- repeating words
- throat clearing
- singing
- mimicking the sounds of animals & objects
- humming
- talking to yourself
- whistling

Circle the ones you are doing, cross out the ones you're not & add more if you want to.

50+ Sensory Icks

Sensory Icks Tier List

Tactile

wet hair on neck

long nails

clothing tags

sweating in fuzzy sweater

tight clothes

dry skin

chalky textures

sticky hands

nylon socks

light touch on arms

sweat

wet feet

dust on fingers

metal straws

bare feet

wet surfaces

seams & stitches

itchy clothes

velvet

jeans

microfiber

Visual

screens in the dark

cold white lights

flashing lights

clutter

glare

flickering lights

direct sunlight

fluorescent lights

neon colors

busy patterns

Add your own:

Taste & Smell

car air freshener

bleach

carbonated drinks

artificial sweeteners

other people's perfumes

wet food

vinegar

anything spicy

minty toothpaste

cigarette smoke

Auditory

teeth on metal

vacuum cleaners

balloons popping

high-pitched voices

the sound of certain words

dish clangs to dish

sirens

chewing

fire alarm

metal on glass

water from tap

styrofoam

metal on metal

hand dryers

nails on blackboard

whisper

multiple people talking at once

drills

Get your colored pencils and color the words as you feel:

I'm okay with it

Depends on the day

Please no

AbSoLuTeLy NOT

Autism & Asking for Help

Even in an accepting environment, asking for help can be hard for autistic people.
Here are a few reasons why.

Autism & Asking for Help
Why so Hard?

Not being able to identify
sensory triggers, emotions, physical pain

so you can't tell
why you need help in the first place.

Autism & Asking for Help
Why so Hard?

Being able to identify
what the problem is

but when you're overwhelmed,
you might not be able to talk
or ask for help.

What I wish people understood without me having to explain it...

Autism & Asking for Help
Why so Hard?

Masking/ anxiety/ being overwhelmed/ surviving takes up so much space in your head

that you can identify the triggers only AFTER you had a meltdown/ shutdown/ minor sensory overload.

People, places, situations, or activities where I usually notice my triggers only afterward...

Autism & Asking for Help
Why so Hard?

Struggling and you
need help

but thinking that it's normal because
that is how it has always been

Write or draw your own 'I thought...' moments.

Autism & Asking for Help
Why so Hard?

Self-gaslighting or

being too scared to ask for help

because your
basic needs were dismissed before.

Things I'd tell a friend instead...

Autism & Asking for Help
Why so Hard?

Realizing that you have a problem

but starting to think about where the exact line is between it's OK and it's not OK to ask for help. This whole thought process just makes you even more overwhelmed.

It's okay if
I need help...

Autism & Daily Routine

Why can it be so exhausting?
What can help?

Being so completely immersed in your current activity or environment—and all the sensory input—

that

transitions

can feel like sudden shocks.

Build your own

Transition Toolkit

Tick the ideas you like. Add notes or doodles!

☐ Deep breaths

☐ To-do list

Other:

☐ Timer

☐ Music

☐ Reminders

☐ Preparing ahead

☐ Stretching

Other:

Other:

☐ Breaks

☐ I-have-done list

Autism & Daily Routine

When **too many steps come all at once**, it can feel impossible to know where to start—like the brain just shuts off.

Just one step at a time.
One routine card.
That might be enough.

You've woken up somewhere exciting...

You're in your favorite fictional world, a cozy forest cabin, a magical castle, a beach house, or a place you've invented. What does your routine look like? Write, doodle, or collage.

Autism & Daily Routine

Unexpected changes
can cause
extreme overwhelm,
shutdowns or meltdowns

because when one thing changes,
it can feel like everything
chaotically changes with it,
like a full system breakdown.

Sometimes unexpected changes lead to an even better path.

Can you think of a time when something turned out better than the original plan?

Autism & Decision-Making

It can feel like there is an ocean of options and you have to choose and pick up one perfect drop.

It's overwhelming.

Oh no. Someone's watching, waiting for you to decide—right now. But how can you think at all when your brain freezes and every single eye is on you?

"Well, it's only 2 options now and this decision is not important at all. It must be easier, right?
Right?"
Uhm, now it feels like both options have an ocean of perfect reasons why they would be the best choice.
so I am just stuck analyzing the simplest question for hours.

Which decisions get you stuck?

- [ ] What to wear
- [ ] What to eat
- [ ] Which clothes to buy
- [ ] Which size to order
- [ ] What to watch
- [ ] What to do in your free time
- [ ] What to do first
- [ ] What message to send
- [ ] Which mug or plate to use
- [ ] Where to go
- [ ] What to reply

Write, doodle, or collage your own examples.

Recovering from a meltdown, shutdown or a day full of autistic masking can also make you completely freeze if there is any decision to make.

Not being able to identify feelings, to tell if you're hungry or thirsty can also make decisions even harder.

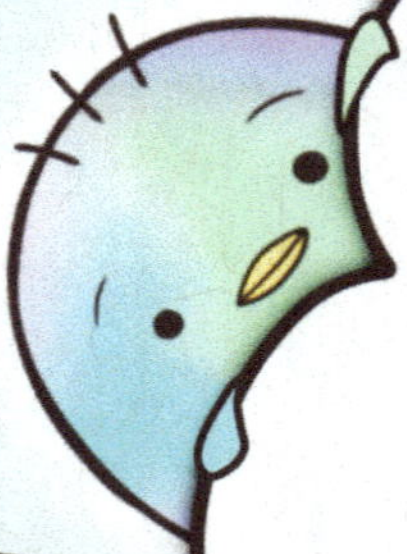

All these things can make daily routines, eating, dressing up, etc., extremely hard since you need to make hundreds of small decisions every single day.

When do decisions become harder?

Write, draw, doodle, or collage about the times when decisions feel harder.

Autism & Decision-Making

A few tips that might help

- Be patient with yourself
- Take your time
- Start with just one step that feels the easiest for you
- Talk about it even if it is just for yourself
- Draw or write down the options
- Use playful visual tools to ease overwhelm and lower the pressure

Think about a time when you finally made a decision.
What helped you get unstuck?
Maybe it was deciding what to wear, what to eat, what to buy, where to go, or something completely different.

Autism Mood Chart
just a few
just for fun
What is your current mood?
fidget toy play
special interest fun
overwhelmed
stimming
All feelings are welcome
sensory avoiding
sensory seeking
low energy day
hyperfocus loop
What is your current mood?

Anytime you come to this page, add your current mood. Words, emojis, and doodles are welcome.

Autism & Waiting Anxiety

Autism & Waiting

Difficulties in understanding the concept of time

If 5 hours can fly by without you noticing when you're in hyperfocus, but 2 minutes can feel like forever when you're overstimulated, planning and trying to see time as linear can be extremely hard.

You might find it helpful to use **visual timers**, or to build **small routines** into your waiting time that you can repeat whenever you need them.

What makes time fly by for you? Write, doodle, add stickers, or make a collage.

Autism & Waiting

Being understimulated

Not enough sensory or mental stimulation, leading to feelings of restlessness, frustration, and being stuck.

What helps me wait?

Waiting for a bus that keeps getting delayed.. .. ..

Waiting for someone who said, 'I'll be there in 5 minutes.'.. .. ..

Waiting for a text back... .. ..

Someone says, 'I'll tell you tomorrow.'.. .. ..

Waiting at home for an afternoon appointment.. .. ..

Waiting in a waiting room... .. ..

Waiting in a long queue in a grocery store.. .. ..

Waiting for someone to finish talking before you can leave... .. ..

1. Music
2. Fidget toy
3. Plushie
4. Water & Snack
5. Crossword
6. Book
7. Call someone
8. Walk around
9. Notebook & pen
10. Other:

Choose one or more for each situation.

Autism & Waiting

Being overstimulated

Too much noise, lights, crowds, or any small trigger that you are sensitive to.

Thank you for helping me!
I'm overwhelmed, but still need to wait for 30 mins. What would you do?

Autism & Waiting

Uncertainty overload

Waiting can feel even more overwhelming if you don't know how long to wait, or if the waiting time changes. All those uncertainties can add up and be just too much.

What can help?
Visual timers, comfort items, breathing exercises, and other small, relaxing activities.

What can help?

accommodations for sensory ease

small routines

relaxing activities

planning in advance

gently moving around

breathing exercises

visual timers

self-compassion

Build Your Perfect Waiting Spot

What are you waiting for? It can be realistic or fictional.

.. ..

Tick one or more from each.

Seat
- ☐ Beanbag
- ☐ Soft chair
- ☐ Window seat
- ☐ Floor

Colors
- ☐ Earthy tones
- ☐ Pastel rainbow
- ☐ One color

Room
- ☐ Plants
- ☐ Blank walls
- ☐ Cozy decor
- ☐ Lots of books

Lighting
- ☐ Bright lamp
- ☐ Night sky projector
- ☐ Fairy lights

People
- ☐ Alone
- ☐ A safe person
- ☐ Quiet crowd

Sounds
- ☐ Silence
- ☐ Music
- ☐ Nature sounds
- ☐ Brown noise

Vibe
- ☐ Castle
- ☐ Beach
- ☐ Fairy
- ☐ Forest
- ☐ Modern

Bonus
- ☐ Blanket
- ☐ Plushie
- ☐ Fidget toy
- ☐ Snack
- ☐ Drink

Now bring your waiting spot to life! Add colors, doodles, stickers, or pictures.

Autism & Being Exhausted

Autism
&Being
Exhausted

Dealing with change because if one thing changes, all the related things will change, and all of a sudden seeing everything in its full complexity is exhausting.

What helps when plans change?

- [ ] Extra time
- [ ] Knowing in advance
- [ ] A backup plan
- [ ] A familiar person
- [ ] Comfort items
- [ ] Information
- [ ] Taking a break
- [ ] Something else...

List, doodle, or draw your examples.

Autism & Being Exhausted

Dealing with sensory issues,

e.g., lights, sounds, textures, etc.

Battery Drainers & Chargers

Doodle, name or collage all the sensory things that drain or charge your battery. Tiny things count too.

Autism & Being Exhausted

Completing simple tasks with executive function issues.

Things that sometimes
feel huge to me.

Autism &Being Exhausted

A high level of empathy but not knowing what to do with it or how to express it.

E.g., getting to know that a bad little thing happened to a stranger, and then you can't think of anything else all day. Or your friend is sad and you wanna help but have no idea how.

Things I'm good at helping with...

When I want to help...

Things I often don't know how to help with...

Things I can't help with...

Autism &Being Exhausted

Hyperfixation especially when you want to get out of it, but you have no idea how.

Brain Loops

What keeps your brain going in circles for hours?

Research rabbit holes. Tiny decisions. Perfecting things. Replaying conversations. Planning. Small details.

Autism & Being Exhausted

Suddenly having so many new creative ideas that you feel like you might explode.

Ideas. Dreams. Half-finished projects. Random thoughts.

Empty your brain onto this page.

Autistic Meltdown

How to Help

An Autistic Meltdown

...

is NOT a temper tantrum

is the result of some sort of overload

does NOT have a goal

is NOT intentional

can happen with or without people around

does NOT want to hurt anyone

makes an autistic person vulnerable

I'd like you to know...

about my meltdowns, shutdowns & sensory overloads

I wish people knew that I...

Sometimes I need...

Please don't...

One thing that makes a big difference is...

Autistic Meltdown

How to Help

Autistic Meltdown

How to Help

Be kind.

If you stay calm and say a few kind words, it can mean a world of difference, even if you don't get any reaction since the meltdown still goes on.

The person will feel your compassion.

People care about you

Collect moments of warmth and care during overwhelming situations.
Small acts of kindness you're grateful for.

Autistic Meltdown

How to Help

Don't ask 'What's wrong?'

This question can be extremely overwhelming for someone having an autistic meltdown.

1. it's an open-ended question.
2. for many autistic people, it's hard to identify feelings and their causes, especially during a meltdown.

Autistic Meltdown

How to Help

Make sure that the room is sensory friendly.

Turn down any bright lights or loud noises that can be triggering. If it's not possible, then help to find a way out of the place or situation.

Accept, don't fight.

Don't try to fight with the meltdown, don't try to stop it because you can't.
Don't ask to stop it either because it will only increase the pressure and the meltdown will get worse.

Accept that it is happening.
It's what helps the most and it helps a lot.

During an autistic meltdown, you might face challanges that you have no idea how to handle. Also, keep in mind that with co-occurring conditions, a meltdown might not be 'just' an autistic meltdown.

Always ask for professional help if needed.

Draw it. Write it. Doodle it. Add stickers. Or don't.

Stimming is natural
Your special interests are vital
Your strengths are unique
Your needs are important
Autistic Reminders
All kinds of communication are valid
You are loved
Resting is productive
The world needs you
Meltdowns are not your fault

Add your own reminders.
Draw. Write. Doodle. Add stickers, photos, memories, or anything that makes you feel good about yourself.

Autistic NON-Deficits

Autistic Non-Deficits

Autistic interests
are anything
but 'narrow' or 'restricted'

They can be incredibly broad, limitless, and inexhaustible. But only if you can see those magical little details, complexity and the infinite possibilities that even the smallest thing in the world can offer.

10 Fun Facts

About My Special Interest

1.

2.

3.

4.

5.

6.

7.

8.

9.

10.

Autistic Non-Deficits

Repetitive playing & happy stimming are not pointless.

It's about having fun and feeling the same calming, joyful, refreshing emotions over and over again. It might seem pointless from the outside because others might not see the richness and beauty of those little things that can be a complex and vivid experience for an autistic person.

Again & again

What little things do you happily do over and over again? Maybe it's collecting, sorting, lining things up, or something completely different.

Autistic Non-Deficits

Parallel play

is not about excluding someone

It's about showing love to someone.

It's about feeling a loved one's presence in a calming way.

It's a way of communication, and sometimes it means so much more than words.

Do you enjoy someone's presence while doing your own thing? Make this page your own.

Autistic Non-Deficits

Playing alone

is not a deficit.

It's about fully engaging with something.
It's like submerging into one's own magical world.

Alone Time

When do you need it?
What do you do when you're alone?
Add stickers, colors, or doodles to show your vibe.

Autistic Non-Deficits

Autistic joy
is never pointless.

It's unique. It's beautiful just as
YOU ARE.

Trace around your hand.
Fill it with all the good things you see in yourself.

One book down.
More to come.

Explore more autism tools at
lilpenguinstudios.com

- Communication Cards
- Decision Kit
- Daily Routine Kit
- Calm-Down Kit
- Feelings Kit
- Planner Kit
- Travel Kit

About the author

Hi, I'm Réka,
an autistic artist from Hungary.

I hand-drew and wrote every page
in this book with lots of care.

Thank you for
spending time with
LiL Penguin and me.

Meet LiL Penguin's Crew

LiL Penguin

- happily flaps her wings every time she sees you
- loves plushies & everything soft and fluffy
- collects erasers
- knows that healing takes time

Pogi the frog could spend hours jumping around, stimming in water & talking about water lilies.

Zizi the axolotl loves fairy lights and being surrounded by cuddly things.

Linzer the unicorn is fascinated by butterflies, math & ballet. Sees the beauty in the smallest things.

Gofri the capybara likes slow days, cloud-gazing and quiet company.

Kex is the sweetest dino ever. His favorite food is Mac & cheese.

Sherbow the shark collects smooth rocks and always keeps one in his pocket.

Sendo is a sleepy little cat who is just there for you. No words needed.

Boocta the cat secretly wishes every month was October.

Coogloaf the ghost finds comfort in floating around cozy places.

Kifli the dog gets excited about all kinds of vehicles, crunchy leaves, and the wind on his face.

www.ingramcontent.com/pod-product-compliance
Lightning Source LLC
LaVergne TN
LVHW060547061126
851857LV00017B/1927
9786150275147